Home Time

A BOOK TO ENTERTAIN YOUR CHILD

FANCY DRESS

Written and compiled by Jackie Andrews
Illustrated by Lesley Smith and Anne Parsons

Home Time is a series of six books, each designed to give the busy parent bright ideas!
Each chosen item has been tested with children of various ages with much success.
You will find fresh ideas, with clear instructions, to interest and entertain your child
throughout the year, in any weather, using only basic materials or ingredients.

HENDERSON
PUBLISHING PLC

FANCY DRESS

THE FUN OF FANCY DRESS

Children love to dress up and don't really need an excuse for it. Playing out adult roles and slipping into a fantasy world with the help of just a few props and items of clothing is as important to their development as eating a balanced diet. But they don't need to wait for the school play, Halloween, or a costume party - it's a great way to spend a rainy day indoors, or having fun with friends in the back garden.

Don't imagine that you need to spend back-breaking hours over your sewing machine, putting something complex together. Most of the ideas in this book are quick and cheap, relying more on staples and glue than fancy pattern construction. But it helps if you have already collected a few items beforehand, and these are mentioned, too. When Dressing-Up is the name of the game, your children won't want to have to wait ages for you to put a costume together for them.

Learn to adapt ideas. If you can't come up with just the costume that's needed, then ask your children for ideas: you might be surprised by the scope of their ingenuity. With just a few minor changes, for instance, Puss in Boots can become one of the Three Musketeers!

★ A Quick Tip ★

In order to save you time, we have highlighted the articles or accessories to be used for each costume. Each article carries this symbol ★. When you need ideas in a hurry, you can skim through the pages and, pick out the necessary articles ★ at a glance. Only when you decide on a certain costume, do you then need to read the fuller descriptions and detail on that page.

A FEW BASICS

A dressing-up box is your first priority: somewhere practical and accessible to store all those wonderful items of clothing and fabric. A large cardboard box will do, or a bottom drawer, an old laundry basket, or an Ottoman (but not one with a heavy lid which might fall on unsuspecting fingers).

Into this goes a variety of discarded clothing and accessories, which you can add to over the years. It's important that young children understand that these are play things: anything else is strictly out of bounds if you don't want them playing with your best clothes and jewellery!

It pays to become familiar with your local charity shop. Often you will be able to find unusual items of clothing and accessories for a cheap price. But be open-minded: it's not only clothes that make good costumes. Lace and velveteen curtains make fabulous robes for kings, queens or brides; tablecloths, funny shoes, hats, scarves, shawls, beads, feathers, evening bags and frilly shirts are all potentially useful. Your only limitation is the size of your storage space!

Look around the house for items or materials which might make useful props: black plastic refuse bags, paper carrier bags, string, cardboard tubes, wire coat hangers, aluminium foil, empty fabric-softener bottles, towels and corrugated cardboard. Start saving those things which you once threw away, including egg cartons, plastic containers, cardboard, beads, buttons, cork. The list is endless, but you'll see in the instructions for the costumes which follow, that anything goes.

STAND BYS

Children left to play on their own won't need much more than the clothes and accessories, and it's safest to leave it at that, especially with younger ones. However, if you are helping them create something more special, then here are a few things which you will find useful:

- all purpose, non-toxic glue
- glue used for false eyelashes (good for beards and moustaches)
- all purpose scissors
- safety pins
- double-sided tape
- brown parcel tape
- masking tape
- craft knife
- face paints

SAFETY NOTES

- Some items (plastic bags, staples, etc.) can be hazardous. Use them with caution with younger children.

- Make sure the costume enables freedom of movement, that the child can walk without tripping, eat and drink, and visit the bathroom without too many problems.

- If the weather is cold, ensure that the costume provides sufficient warmth.

- For night-time costume parties, stick a few reflective patches on dark costumes to help make children visible.

- Fasten headgear securely so it does not fall over your child's eyes. Use face paint rather than masks on younger children.

STORIES AND PANTO: GOODIES AND BADDIES

SNOW WHITE

This classic heroine just needs
★ **an oversized yellow skirt**
★ **a white blouse with puffed sleeves** ★ **a skinny blue vest or tank-top.**

Alternatively, make sleeves out of white or blue crepe paper and attach them with double-sided tape to the armholes of the tank top.

Make up
A little make-up goes a long way to making children feel they are really the character they are playing, and anyway they just love to fool around with face paints and cosmetics.
Snow White could do with some pink cheeks and bright red lips.

Cover ★ **a head band** with red ribbon or crepe paper and attach a large bow on the top of it.

If your heroine doesn't have dark hair (black is best to show off her porcelain skin and red lips), then make a quick wig with ★ **curly black paper strips** (see page 45).

Tip: to make a long skirt stand out, fill a pillow case with crumpled newspaper. Pin the open end. Attach to the underside of the skirt, at the waistband.
Two stuffed pillow cases, one on each hip, make a good bustle for a Hanoverian dress.

ALADDIN

Not an ideal costume for a cold night. If necessary, your child could wear a long-sleeved t-shirt or leotard as well. ★ **An oversized pair of sweatpants** with elasticated ankles make good harem trousers.
Add ★ **a wide sash** - made from a long scarf - and top them off with ★ **a short waistcoat.**

Although Aladdin would have been barefoot, for practical purposes your character can wear ★ **sandals.** Those with a thong between the toes are just the thing.

You can make him ★ **a fez hat** out of card or the bottom of a large lemonade bottle, tied on with fine elastic.

He needs ★ **a lamp,** too, but you might have to substitute a teapot or lantern.

GENIE

A colourful character, who needs colourful clothes.
Use ★ **a bright towel** for the turban, fastened with a safety pin and with ★ **a fancy brooch and feathers** (real or paper) at the front.

Hang ★ **a large brass curtain ring** from one ear (on a loop of flesh-coloured cotton) and fashion ★ **a curly black beard** out of paper to stick on the chin with eyelash glue or a small piece of double-sided tape. ★ **A pair of sandals** or rubber beach shoes with thongs complete the outfit.

★ **A bright red or blue vest or t-shirt** (close-fitting) makes a suitable top, and you can use ★ **oversized sweatpants** for the harem pants (see Aladdin) or, for a brighter effect, two squares of colourful fabric (or scarves) knotted together at the waist and tied round the ankles, worn over cycle shorts. ★ **A long silky scarf** makes a sash at the waist.
Make ★ **two wrist cuffs** out of gold-covered stiff paper or card, fastened with tape.

WICKED WITCH

Black plastic rubbish bags come into their own for the Wicked Witch. Wearing ★ **a black t-shirt or leotard and leggings** as a base, make a skirt out of ★ **two or more rubbish bags**, cut to the right length to reach the ankles. Staple the waist into gathers and tie in place with ★ **a long strip of black plastic** over double-sided tape to cover the staples.

Make a cape out of ★ **another black rubbish bag,** gathered at the neck with ★ **a ribbon** to create a collar effect. Decorate both with ★ **cut-out, or novelty rubber bats, spiders, etc.**

You need to make ★ **a witch's hat** (see page **43**), with strings of straggly grey hair attached to the inside rim, made from ★ **ravelled wool.** ★ **A pair of old black gloves** with stick-on giant black fingernails make impressive, spooky hands.

Have fun creating a masterly wicked face with face paints, with stuck-on warts (★ **screwed-up plasters** look good) and a huge nose made from modelling clay.

Make a broomstick from ★ **a wooden handle and twigs** bound tightly round it, and give the witch a stuffed toy cat if possible (her 'familiar') - to trail behind her on a lead or stuff under her arm.

PUSS IN BOOTS

★ **The hat and boots** are the key items here. Puss can be given some creative make-up with face paints (see page **48**). He needs ★ **a fancy shirt with lace cuffs** (make these out of stiff paper and white doily lace),

★ **a short cloak** made from a curtain gathered at the neck into a tie ribbon, and ★ **pants** tied with a cummerbund (a colourful scarf or piece of fabric) and tucked into the tops of the boots.

Give ★ **ordinary boots** (even Wellingtons if you're pushed) a romantic touch by adding wide cuffs made from stiff fabric (like brocade) or crepe paper in a suitable colour and trimmed with more doily lace. Fix the cuffs to the inside of the boots with tape and attach bows to the sides for additional panache. Stick on over-sized buckles made from card covered with aluminium foil. Slip hands into ★ **fur gloves** if you have them, otherwise dark ones.

> **Tip:** Puss is a good basic costume for a variety of others, such as a Musketeer, Highwayman (add a mask and a pistol in his belt), or Captain Hook (see page **15**).

You can make Puss ★ **a wide-brimmed hat** (see page **44**), which needs to be trimmed with flamboyant feathers (made out of paper if necessary) and a band.

Older children could add a few black paper whiskers, stuck to the cheeks with eyelash glue, to complete the character.

FANTASTIC MR. FOX

Roald Dahl's wily, debonair character is ideally played by someone tall, slim and red-haired, but it's not difficult to improvise.

His basic costume is ★ **a white shirt** ★ **waistcoat** ★ **hunting jacket** (make some tucks in a loose-fitting jacket if you don't have anything more suitable) and ★ **beige trousers** tucked into ★ **boots** (or thick, black knee-socks), and ★ **a bright spotted** scarf in his neck. ★ **A pair of brown gloves** will save you having to disguise the hands.

Fox's tail needs to look as if it has been shot away. Make some large circles of orange crepe paper, snipped round the edges to make a fringe, and stick them on top of each other. Attach to back of Fox's coat or pants, where they will be seen. Make a smaller circle of black crepe paper fringing to stick in the centre of the others.

Now make up Fox's face with face paints (as shown on page **48**), and two foxy ears in craft paper attached to a head band covered in orange /brown paper.

If you prefer, you can fashion a painted mask instead (see page **42**).

QUEEN (OR KNAVE) OF HEARTS

It's easy to adapt this unisex costume with ★ **leggings** for the Knave, ★ or **a long red skirt** for the Queen, worn with ★ **a red or black polo-necked jumper.** They can both carry the obligatory ★ **tray of jam tarts,** though if you use real ones it's doubtful whether they'll hang on to them long!

The key items are ★ **the tabards, collars and hats,** which are all made from card or craft paper, and their colourful 'card' faces made with face paints (see page **48**).

The hat is simply a circle of red card, slit to the middle to form a shallow cone. Attach a wide white rim, and decorate with an abundance of red hearts

CAPED CRUSADER

Caped Crusaders have been with us a good many years, in popular comics and TV cartoon adventures. Whether it's Superman, Batman or Spiderman, their costumes are basically the same: ★ **a long-sleeved, tight-fitting t-shirt or leotard,** ★ **leggings** and ★ **contrasting running shorts.** Only the colour distinguishes them. The chest panel, with a stylised monogram (you can use your own), can be made from a triangle of paper either pinned or stuck with double-sided tape.

★ **A colourful plastic bag, curtain or bath-towel** makes a good cloak, gathered at the neck and fastened with either tape or a safety pin. Don't forget to stick another monogram on the back.

★ **A belt** around the waist, in another contrasting colour, completes the picture. Wear ★ **knee-length socks** over leggings to look like tight-fitting boots, or pull them over slim shoes so that the child can walk outside in them.

Up, up and away!

MASKED MENACE

This one is supposed to be sinister, so it's best to use colours like red or black in the costume. A simple mask can be made from ★ **a cut-off sleeve from a t-shirt**, with two holes cut for the eyes and a notch for the nose.

The Menace needs ★ **a sash or leather belt** from which can hang a cardboard cutlass or sword, ★ **black gloves and socks** pulled up over the leggings to look like boots.

Use ★ **a black rubbish bag** for a cape (see Wicked Witch, page **9**) and ★ **black or red leggings** and ★ **t-shirt**.

Some furtive peering over a swished cloak is necessary to give the character the right charisma!

CAPTAIN HOOK

Captain Hook's costume can follow the same lines as Puss in Boots (see page **10**) for the ★ **shirt**, ★ **pants**, ★ **hat** and ★ **boots**. In addition, he needs a long coat with wide cuffs - a shortened dressing-gown is ideal - and a sword hanger across his chest (a leather belt or long sash from a fabric remnant will do).

His hook can be made from ★ **a wire coat hanger hook** (see diagram)

pushed into ★ a **large paper or foam cup.** Cover both with foil. He holds onto the base of the hook under the cup.

See page **47** for how to make his sword. Pencil in some bushy black eyebrows and attach two thin, black paper moustachios under his nose with eyelash glue. He now needs to practise scowling and gnashing his teeth.

> "Shiver me timbers and buckle me swashes!"

INDY JONES

A rugged expression and dusty clothes go halfway to making this modern-day adventure hero. He needs ★ **an open-necked khaki shirt**, ★ **baggy khaki trousers** - torn in a few places - ★ **rolled socks** and ★ **climbing boots**. The hat needs to be ★ **a battered bush hat** (or as near as you can get - see page **43** for ideas) with a stained band round it. You can have fun giving everything a dusty, grimy, well-worn look (don't forget to cake the boots in mud!). Cold, strong tea makes realistic sweat stains!

Over these he needs ★ **a leather belt** hung with cardboard knives, gadgets (rifled from the kitchen drawer) and, of course, his bullwhip (an old skipping rope dyed dark brown is just the thing).

Because he is a rugged, outdoor type, a liberal sweep of bronzing powder over forehead, cheeks, nose, and neck (where the shirt opens), and grey designer shadow (made by stippling and smudging a grey/black eye pencil) around mouth and jaws should create the right illusion. Brush bronzer over backs of hands and wrists, too.

ROBIN HOOD

A perennial favourite, and one which has undergone a number of transformations over the years with each new large and small screen interpretation of the original legend. He remains basically, however, a macho 12th century woodsman with a flair for fancy archery.

Robin's foundation costume needs to be ★ **brown pants or leggings**, tucked into ★ **thick sock 'boots'** ★ **a brown or green shirt**, ★ **leather belt** with a dagger, sword (see page **47**) and money purse, and another belt hung across one shoulder to the opposite hip carrying a quiver of arrows.

Make a jaunty, brown-paper hat with a feather (see page **44**), and throw ★ **a cape** (a dark-coloured curtain, for instance) loosely round his shoulders. A staff in one hand or his longbow slung over one shoulder should complete the desired effect.

This could be a duo tableau with Maid Marian. (See the Medieval Princess on page **20**). Just add ★ **a low-slung belt** with a dagger - Marian was well versed in looking after herself - and use a plain headband over a plain veil instead of a coronet or high hat.

A GANGSTER
AND HIS MOLL

Time to dig out that ★ **old pinstripe suit!** Although it should be oversized, you might have to make some judicious tucks or shortening of sleeves and trousers to make it practical to wear.

You could also give him thin moustaches drawn with eyeliner pencil.

Underneath, it needs ★ **a dark shirt** with ★ **a white (or very light) tie.**

The ultimate accessories are ★ **a fedora,** pulled down over one mean eye, and either ★ **a toy machine gun** or - better still- ★ **a violin case.** If you don't have a hat, then slick the gangster's hair down with styling gel.

Moll could wear ★ **a too-big silky slip**, with ★ **a feather boa** wrapped round her neck and shoulders. (If it's a cold day, then add a short cardigan). Lots of ★ **sparkly jewellery** (see page **46**), ★ **light opaque tights** and ★ **strappy shoes**.

Give cheeks a dab of blusher, a dusting of powder on the face, and bright red lips. If her head isn't naturally covered in bubbly curls, then add a few with heated rollers or a hot brush. Straight hair could be given the Veronica Lake treatment - a side parting and a heavy fall over one eye.

"Hey, Kid, how 'bout a dance?"

To be perfectly in character, she needs to chew gum - real or imaginary - and occasionally gaze into a powder compact to check her shiny nose. She views the world through half-closed, bored eyes. If she and the gangster are in tandem, then Moll needs to drape herself over the gangster's shoulder seductively.

MEDIEVAL PRINCESS

★ **An old pair of brocade curtains** is ideal for this costume. Use one for the top and gather the other into a skirt (stapling the folds will save you time) making it full at the front (it was considered beautiful to look pregnant in those days), with a train behind. You'll probably need to adjust the front hem so that the princess doesn't fall over it when she walks.

Draw the sleeves and sides with very generous seam allowances. At the centre, make a slit for her head. Close the side seams, from wrist to waist, by machine, safety pins or double-sided tape.

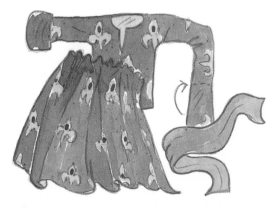

Turn back the sleeve overhang to her wrists, making cuffs. Attach the gathered skirt to the bodice so that it sits very high - almost to the armpits - and wrap ★ **a scarf** cummerbund where the two join.

Fold the second curtain over lengthways: it needs to be long enough to hang over each hand and stretch across the shoulders (measuring is best done on the floor with your victim lying with her arms stretched out).

For my lady's hat, make a tall dunce's hat out of stiff paper (embossed wallpaper would be good), leaving a hole at the top. Now take ★ **a long chiffon scarf** (you might need to put two together), wrap it under her chin, up through the hat and out of the small hole, so that it trails from the end of the hat.

Secure the base of the hat with hair grips. (If it still falls off, then attach fine elastic to each side of the hat and take it round her chin. Conceal with the chiffon scarf.)

Make some bold, heavy jewellery (see page **46**) and if your princess wants to be really regal, add a gold coronet round the base of her pointed hat and some gold slippers on her feet.

A few hours' posture practise with books on head should create the right royal impression.

COURT JESTER

The real court jesters were very musical, and good acrobats and jugglers. All-round entertainment was the name of their game.

Look for bright colours: ★ **shiny tights or leggings** topped with ★ **an oversized shirt** (especially a multicoloured rugby shirt) with its collar removed. Make ★ **a shoulder cape** out of a circle of crepe paper or colourful fabric, and the hat out of crepe paper or felt, following the pattern below.

The jester's props can be juggling balls, a stick with a balloon on a string (instead of a pig's bladder, which is what they used to use), and perhaps a copy of a joke book tucked cheekily into a pocket or waistband. Shoes need to be flat and simple, or else use brightly coloured socks.

★ **A few small bells** - the kind found on pet collars - strung from the hat, tunic or cape, complete this extrovert character.

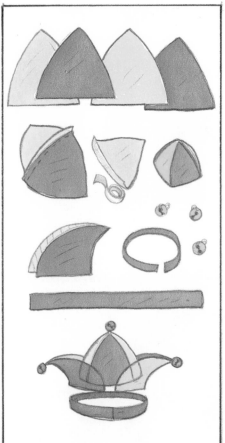

KINGS & QUEENS

This can be a quick, five-minute costume or something more elaborate, depending on your child's needs. Children just love to parade around regally, issuing royal decrees to everyone!

★ **A brocade curtain** gathered at the neck and allowed to trail behind, is the main feature: tunic (★ **oversized shirt**) and ★ **leggings** for the king; ★ **long skirt** and ★ **frilly blouse** for the queen. ★ **A wide sash**, purple ideally, across the chest, with fancy rosette pinned on the robe, just below the shoulder.

Make an elegant crown out of foiled card and Christmas tinsel, or simply yellow paper stuck with sweet-paper jewels.

Needs a very upright carriage and a stiff wave.

MERLIN

This ancient magician needs an air of mystery about him, tinged with just a little fusty eccentricity. Everyone knows that serious magicians are too absorbed in their craft to worry about respectability.

A dark, dusty robe (made from ★ **an old bed sheet** dyed black) is a good start, worn over ★ **a black roll-neck shirt** and ★ **black leggings**. Measure shoulder height of child; measure the same distance from the hem of the sheet and fold over (see diagram).

Make a slit in the centre of the fold for Merlin's head.

Fold back the sleeve overhang and pin into place at the wrist. Make two small slits at each side on the waistline and thread a leather belt through, taking it round the waist of the child. Fasten comfortably.

Decorate the robe with stuck-on glitter, stars and crescents and signs of the zodiac - you can be as imaginative as you like!

Make a cone hat (see page **43**) and add some silver stars. Trim the inside of the hat with long, grey hair (made from teased grey wool dusted with talcum powder) and a long beard hanging on thin string with loops for ears, which will sit on the child's chin when the hat is in place. Secure the hat with elastic under the chin (beneath the beard).

Give Merlin a pale face, with grey shadows and powdered eyebrows.

The children can have great fun putting together Merlin's props. A knotty piece of stick makes a good staff; and his book of spells can be made from a cereal box covered and painted to look like a book. An ancient gold medallion hanging on his chest and a magic-looking ring made from balled-up foil chocolate wrappers on a foil-covered band, will also add to his aura of mystique.

THE DRAGON SLAYER (ST. GEORGE)

This guy's squeaky clean - the stuff of heroes. Give him ★ **a white oversized tunic,** ★ **light-coloured leggings or sweatpants** and ★ **boots** (use thick socks if necessary). Over the top he needs ★ **a tabard made from a heavy fabric** (an old cotton damask tablecloth, for instance) with a large, red cross of St George on it.

Make him a large white shield with a similar device, and a very large sword.

His helmet is going to be his focal point. Use an ★ **upturned colander** (or plastic mixing bowl) covered in foil if it's not metal, with a large plume attached. The visor is a piece of card covered with foil and attached with tape at the sides.

For a knight in shining armour, add shoulder plates, leg and armbands made from tinfoil dishes and corrugated card covered in foil or painted with silver paint. ★ **Dish cloths,** sewn together and dyed grey, make good chain mail: fashion them into a hood and a circular cape to wear under the helmet and tabard.

> *Best to keep your young hero away from unsuspecting pets and domestic livestock!*

BALLERINAS

Tutus can be made from a variety of things: you just need the basic top and tights, or leotard. Ballet shoes if you have them, otherwise flat casuals.

Scarf Fairy: you need ★ **a number of chiffon or silk squares** for the skirt, two for the top and two for each shoulder. Knot the scarves in place along another, folded scarf and tie this round the waist. Knot the two scarves at the shoulders and tuck inside the skirt, easing them out a little to make an overhang. You might need to pin the sides under the arms to keep them in place. Attach the remaining scarves at the shoulders to hang down each side of the arms.

For a headdress, take a long chiffon scarf round the forehead and tie at the back, so that the ends fall down behind. Alternatively, if your dancer has long hair which can be put into a topknot, tie the final scarf round this.

Good News: Folded newspaper makes a great tutu, but you'll need plenty of it. Take three sheets of paper and fold them in half to make six layers. Cut the open edges into zig-zags. Now fold the sheets into 3-inch (7.5 cm) concertina folds, stapled together as shown. Repeat the process, stapling the sheets together until they are long enough to reach round the ballerina's waist. Tape the edges together.

Attach the tutu to the dancer's leotard with safety pins to keep it in place. A newspaper flower attached to a headband completes the outfit.

Bubblewrap Queen: bubblewrap is lightweight and bulky, so it stands out nicely from the waist, but still looks fairly ethereal. Following the instructions for the newspaper tutu, use a length of bubblewrap instead. It can be tacked loosely to length of elastic to circle the waist.

Take small pieces of bubblewrap (about 15" x 3" or 38 x 7.5cm) to make roses to pin in the hair and round neckline, or to simply make a gathered band for a hair knot.

POLICEMEN AND WOMEN

Nowadays there's little to distinguish the men from the gals in police work, though in the UK, policewomen might be seen wearing straight skirts. It's the accessories which are fun - the pretend communicator pinned to the epaulette; note pad, whistle, identity card, handcuffs and - if you have one - an attack-trained toy dog to haul around.

The basic U.K. uniform is the same for both - ★ **white shirt with epaulettes** (sew on cotton strips if necessary) sporting their number in silver numerals made from foil-backed card (the kind you find as lids to ready meals). ★ **Dark trousers** and ★ **tie.** Girls should wear black or navy tights if they wear a skirt. You'll probably need to find suitable hats (flat tops for drivers, with chequered bands) from a toy shop.

U.S. cops are much more hard-bitten. ★ **Uniforms** are generally blue (you could get away with denim) with ★ **dark ties** and ★ **blue trousers/slacks.** They each need ★ **a leather belt** hung with all the above accessories, plus a rounders bat and a holster for a gun slung at the back (which you could make from stiff, dark-brown paper if necessary). You need to make two Police Dept. badges: one for the shirt pocket and the other for the front of the cap.

Flexing the knees and muttering "Hello, hello, hello" is a bit passé now, but you could try **"POLICE - FREEZE!"** or **"Spread 'em!"** instead.

NATIVE AMERICAN

The cinema has produced a number of Native American heroes in recent years, a far cry from the shrieking scalp-hunters which had become the unfortunate stereotype of these great people.

A basic costume for the boys would be ★ **fringed leggings,** ★ **arm bands,** ★ **strings of fancy beads** and ★ **a decorative headband** round a wig of long, straight black hair made from wool (see page **45**).

A warmer idea would include a ★ **fringed tunic top,** and if you feel very creative, a chieftain's feathered headdress made from paper, with stuck-on paper feathers. Fringes can be made from crepe paper or fabric and stuck on with double-sided tape.

Girls just need ★ **a fringed brown tunic,** which could be decorated with suitable patterns (the research could be fun and instructive) and the decorative headband, with or without a feather. Hair ideally needs to be in two plaits just behind the ears.

Neither need shoes, but if you have some moccasin-type slippers then use those, or strappy leather sandals.

Accessories could include a bow and arrow, belt hung with knife, and bead bracelets.

Use face paints to give very sun-browned colour to the face and exposed skin, with broad bands of yellow, red and white across cheeks and on the forehead.

ASTRONAUT

Start off with ★ **a white sweatsuit** (oversized), ★ **bulky trainers** (or white rubber boots) and ★ **ski gloves.** Add a belt hung with suitable space-type equipment, including ★ **tubing, boxes and packets of dried food** (let your spaceman be creative here). Make a helmet out of ★ **a cardboard box** covered with foil, with a hole cut out for the face, and two semi-circles cut each side to rest on the shoulders.

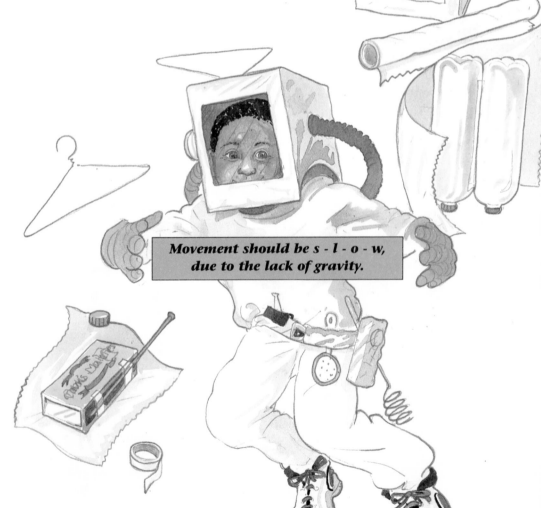

> *Movement should be s - l - o - w,*
> *due to the lack of gravity.*

FLOWER CHILD OF THE 60s

It's Love and Peace time. Dig out those ★ **long, floaty skirts** and ★ **tunic tops,** made from thin cotton or muslin-type fabrics, with ★ **faded jeans or wide cotton trousers** for the boys. Hair needs to be long and straggly, tied round with a band made from a scarf; boys need long moustaches or stuck-on beards. Bare feet or sandals.

Over this basic costume, hang ★ **ropes of beads** (see page 46), bracelets, ankle bracelets and pictures of John Lennon, or ban-the-bomb symbols and perhaps a guitar slung over the back, or tambourine held in one hand. Wear ★ **a pair of steel-rimmed 'granny' glasses** (but not if they contain strong lenses) or improvise a pair in thin, soft wire.

Go to town with your face paints, creating flower tattoos for arms, hands, feet and face - especially a flower or two on the cheek.

If your Flower Child doesn't want to sing or dance, then an alternative would be to sit cross-legged and meditate, saying "Right on" and "Peace, brother (sister)" from time to time.

COWBOY OR COWGIRL

Apart from their obligatory ★ **denim jeans,** these ranch hands need ★ **a checked shirt,** ★ **necktie** and ★ **waistcoat** (you can make this from a well-crumpled brown grocery bag - it resembles ancient leather!) ★ **boots** ★ **and a leather belt** with a fancy silver buckle (see page **46**).

No self-respecting cow-puncher would be seen dead without ★ **a hat:** improvise if necessary with anything broad-brimmed, with strings to keep it attached when galloping across the plain (see page **43**).

Girls can dress the same as the boys, or wear ★ **a fringed denim skirt** instead of jeans. Other accessories might include Sheriff or Deputy badge, fringed cuffs (made from brown paper) and a coil of skipping rope for a lariat. ★ **Chaps** (to protect the legs) can be made from two towels attached each side to the belt, the top corners folded over and then the sides pinned down the inside legs.

Both would benefit from a healthy glow of bronzing powder over forehead, cheeks and chin - also backs of hands - to show these are outdoor types.

Toting six-shooters is to be discouraged.

AMERICAN FOOTBALLER

Choose a favourite colour scheme
and try and co-ordinate it
throughout the costume: team
loyalty is big with these macho guys.

The costume is basically
★ **an oversized t-shirt** and
★ **leggings,** worn under
★ **vest** and ★ **cycle shorts,**
and stuffed with ★ **pieces of foam**
strapped to legs, knees and shoulders.

The helmet can be
★ **an upside-
down plastic
mixing bowl
or colander,**
with a paper
grid attached
and the player's
number stuck to
the front.

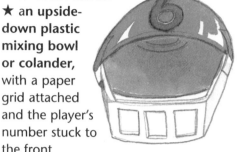

Make large paper numbers
for the front and back of
the vest, and paper stars
or stripes to embellish the
team colours. Complete
with ★ **socks and
trainers.**

*Head down, run in with
the ball and go for it!*

GIANT SANDWICH

In principle, this costume is a giant sandwich board: ★ **two rectangles of card covered** with wide polyester fleece (used for quilting), attached to shoulder straps and worn over ★ **a t-shirt and tights, or leotard.**

Stain the edges of the fleece with strong tea, to look like crusts. You can stick on some paper sesame seeds, too, if you like.

It's your choice what goes into the sandwich, although it's best to avoid runny ingredients like jam or honey, as these are difficult to simulate! You could, for instance, make large slices of cardboard cucumber and tomato, rustle up some crepe paper lettuce and strips of light card painted as streaky bacon. Recruit some help with the painting.

If you're feeling really inventive, the child inside could be dressed as an ingredient - a pink prawn, chicken, or hot chilli, for instance!

PIZZA

Similar to the sandwich, in that it is based on ★ **a large, round board** which hangs on a harness over the shoulders and tied round the waist. ★ **A red t-shirt** and ★ **red leggings** make the best foundation.

Make the base board from two circles of corrugated card, glued with the corrugated sides together. The size of the circle depends on the height of your child: it shouldn't be too big to handle!

Just like a real pizza, build up the layers of colours - red tomato sauce, yellow cheese, etc. - on top of the base board in scraps of fabric, or crepe paper, or painted quilting fleece, ensuring that the edges of the card are completely hidden. Cut out cardboard vegetables, circles of pepperoni, and onion rings (from fleece or foam), painted accordingly. Stick them over your pizza in an appetising arrangement.

Enjoy!

MR. OR MRS. MOP

This costume will cause a lot of laughs, groans - and might even make some people a little thoughtful! It's just as funny for a girl or a boy, but it's important that the boys are themselves - not just dressed up as housewives.

The basic costume is ★ **an old housecoat or apron** over ★ **ancient t-shirt and jeans,** ★ **fluffy slippers** (especially old ones) and ★ **rollers in the hair** (spike the boy's hair into a tousled mess with gel).

Then add as many authentic props as you can find: a 'baby' strapped to front or back; iron, vacuum cleaner, dusters, polish, toy mobile phone (or make one) and perhaps even a toy dog on wheels to pull around are just a few suggestions. Lighter props can be attached to the housecoat with double-sided tape, or stuffed in pockets so that they hang out or are clearly visible.

Complete the look with some dramatic under-eye shadows and a few premature stress lines!

> *The occasional weak, self-sacrificing smile will add authenticity here!*

BUTTERFLY & ANGEL

Although they might look very different, both these characters demand impressive wings.

The angel needs to be dressed in white (★ a **white robe or negligee** is ideal, otherwise use a sheet as for Merlin, page **24**) with perhaps a gold tinsel band round her head, or a halo made of a paper plate (see below).

The butterfly's basic costume is a ★ **leotard and tights, or catsuit** - the brighter, the better. ★ A fluffy-knit top gives her a thorax, and her antennae and curled-up proboscis can be made of ★ **wire** attached to an Alice band.

The wings for both are made from ★ **two wire coat hangers** - the kind that bend easily. Cut and bend them as shown; poke the curved hooks through ★ **white bin liners** (for the angel) or ★ **folded craft paper** (butterfly) taped into position. Trim the edges of the angel's wings with serrated cuts to look like feathers; decorate the butterfly wings how you like.

The hooks should rest comfortably over the shoulders, pinned into position with safety pins so they stay put.

The angel probably doesn't need anything else to reinforce her perfection, but you might like to give the butterfly some dramatic face paintworks.

For an alternative, quick butterfly, more suitable for younger children, attach ★ **two colourful chiffon scarves** by one corner to the neck of her leotard, then attach corners to each wrist, so that when she flaps her arms, the wings float nicely behind.

FROG

This could be Froggy or Kermit on his own, or the other half of a Princess and the Frog Prince duo with the Medieval Princess (page **20**).

★ **A green leotard** and ★ **leggings** provide the body. Make oversized frog feet from ★ **green paper or a green plastic carrier bag**, stuck on to ★ **gloves and sock feet.** Cover head with ★ **a green baseball cap** turned backwards or to the side.

Using face paint, make the face green, but with a wide, smiling mouth.
★ **A pair of oversized glasses** in green-covered card, with painted eyeballs complete the picture.

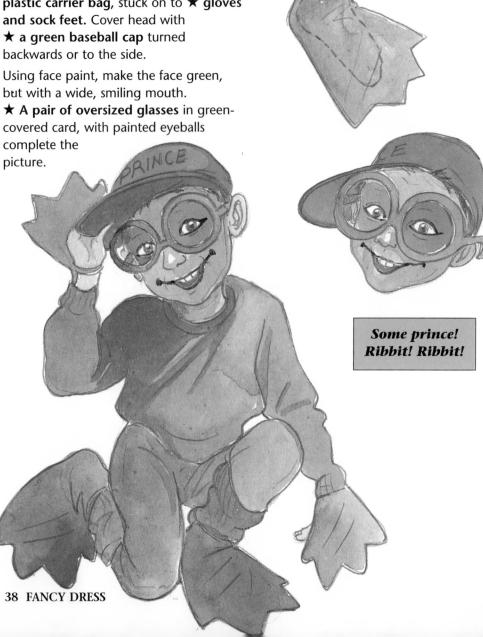

Some prince!
Ribbit! Ribbit!

HEADLESS GHOST

Strictly speaking, this ought to be an historical character: one, like Anne Boleyn, who really did lose her head. But it's an intriguing costume, anyway, and utilising ★ **an old suit** is much easier than putting together something historically accurate.

Start with ★ **a cardboard tube** which fits comfortably over the ghost's head and shoulders. Cut a hole to fit his head through, and curved holes each side to fit over the shoulders. Stuff the top of the tube with ★ **something red** (a towel, tissue paper or fabric). The suit trousers will probably need turning up and clinching in a belt.

Build up the ghost's shoulders with padding (foam, or small cushions), then slip over ★ **one of Dad's shirts and the suit jacket.** The neck of the shirt should hide the cardboard tube, otherwise adjust the red towel. Stuff the sleeves lightly.

Pop ghostie's head through the hole, and fasten the shirt around him. The stuffed sleeves should look to be supporting the 'dismembered' head.

If your child isn't happy with this, you could substitute a painted balloon for the head, attached under one arm of the jacket. Their head remains inside the tube, cut with a slit to see and breath through. Surreal but gruesome!

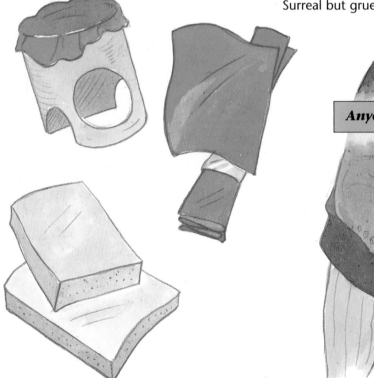

Anyone got an aspirin?

CHARLIE CHAPLIN

It's the duck-like waddle and dead-pan expression that are important to cultivate for a convincing Charlie.

The basic costume comprises
★ **black trousers** and ★ **jacket** (a size too big is best), with
★ **white shirt** (stand the collar up) and ★ **bow tie**, topped with
★ **a bowler hat** (compromise with one from a toy shop if necessary) and
★ **a cane walking stick.** Not forgetting ★ **shiny black shoes.**

Make Charlie's face pale, with dark pencil carefully outlining his eyes to give them that silent-movie look. A small rectangle of black (paper or pencil) under the nose makes his moustache. Tease Charlie's hair to make it look as woolly as possible, or attach black paper curls to the underside of his bowler, so that they frame his face.

CHINESE DRAGON
FOR 3 OR 4 CHILDREN

This needs some team spirit, since the dragon's body comprises three or four children weaving in and out under the bright cloth - ★ **a yellow or red bedspread** would be ideal - with the tallest (and strongest) child carrying the head.

You'll need ★ **plenty of bright red, gold and yellow crepe paper** or foil to decorate the dragon, stuck on with double-sided tape, and ★ **two cardboard boxes** - one approximately 40 cms square, to fit over a child's head and the other roughly the size and shape of a shoe box, to form the snout.

You also need some willing painters and modellers, as well as 'extras' to provide the music.

Make a hole at one end of the bedspread for the head carrier to poke their head through, leaving enough material to cover them up.

Dress the children in ★ **bright tights** to match the colour of the dragon's body, and then get them to practise weaving, bobbing and dancing to some rhythmic percussion music!

MASKS

For those who are not confident about using face paints, these simple masks covering the top half of the face (leaving plenty of room for eating and breathing) can be used on older children for animal and fantasy characters. All you need are craft paper, sticky tape, fine elastic and a clear idea about the character you want to portray.

When measuring the size of the mask, ensure the edges stand out from the side of the face. Tape the elastic to the inside of the mask so that it fits snugly round the head from points each side of the eyes (see diagram). You'll probably have to adjust it a few times until you get it right. Add paper feathers and a beak to a bird mask; whiskers to a cat, a paper mane for a lion, etc.

Paint the tip of the child's nose black or pink, according to the animals portrayed. Covering the mask with tinsel, foil, and silver paint creates a more exotic character.

HATS

Real hats are best for dressing-up, but there are some shapes which you might need to make yourself. Grocery bags, newspaper and card are all good materials to use.

A witch's hat: essentially a cardboard cone (60 x 45 cm) fixed to a circular base (32.5cm diameter) and covered with pieces of black refuse bag, taped into position with black plastic tape. Stick lengths of orange or grey wool round the inside rim of the cone, to hang down as straggly hair. Gently tease the wool so it looks more hair-like.

This cone shape provides the basis for Merlin's hat (stuck with silver stars and moons) and the Medieval Princess (without the brim).

Easy Easter bonnet: cut a large circle of craft paper for the brim of the hat. Cut out a centre circle to fit snugly on the child's head, bending the brim into the shape which looks best. Make a number of colourful flowers and leaves out of tissue or crepe paper and attach them to the hat - especially round the edge of the centre hole, to disguise the head showing through.

This shape can also be adapted for the **Emperor Napoleon:** using black paper, wear the hat sideways to the head and attach ribbons to the top, where the two edges come together. Vive la France!

Basic boater: this basic hat shape can be varied and decorated in any number of ways. Measure the child's head with a piece of string. Cut a circle of card for the brim and a straight piece the measurement of the head: join the two ends with tape to form a circle.

Cut a centre hole in the brim about half-an-inch smaller than the head measurement and snip all round to make tabs to attach the top to the brim. Cut another circle a little larger than the top measurement - snip round the circumference and bend these tabs down to stick them to the hat.

MORE HATS

Puss-in-Boots hat: follow the instructions for the boater, but cut a much larger circle for the brim which will flop round the face. It needs a long chiffon scarf or ribbon tied round the crown and some flamboyant feathers.

Robin Hood hat: this is basically very simple paper folding: fold a sheet of newspaper in half twice; turn up the open edges, pressing firmly, and ease out the hat shape. These turn-backs can be tucked in further to make them more streamlined, and you can tape the rear edges together to make the hat firmer (see diagram).

33"

20"

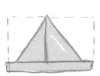

Paint your hat green or brown, then add a jaunty feather, or make one from paper.

Crystal crown: an empty, 2-litre plastic lemonade bottle can be fashioned into an effective crown for a fairy-tale princess. Cut off the top of the bottle at an angle. Cut the sides of the bottle into 8 or 9 deep points, finishing approximately 2" (5cm) from the base.

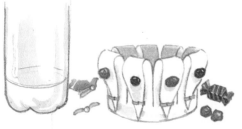

Fold back the points and fix into place with staples or punched holes and paper fasteners. Decorate with paint, glitter or chocolate-wrapper jewels. You might need elastic or hairgrips to keep it in place.

Chef's hat: you'll need strong, white paper for this. Cut a 3" (7.5cm) wide strip long enough to circle the head comfortably, just over the ears. This is the band.

Make the crown with a wider rectangle of paper, folded into regular pleats all round and taped on to the inside of the band. Fasten the back with tape.

WIGS

Proper wigs are not advisable for children to wear to dress up: they tend to be hot, uncomfortable and itchy after a while. Instead, you (and they) can have fun making all kinds of alternatives.

Many of the hats mentioned in the character costumes have woollen hair attached to the brims. This is the easiest 'wig' to produce and, as long as the hat stays in place, the easiest to wear.

Judge's wig: cover cardboard rolls with white or grey paper, pierce holes at each end and thread string through until you have one long strip and two shorter ones. The longer one is worn over the head lengthways, to hang down the back, and the shorter strips are attached to the sides with sticky tape.

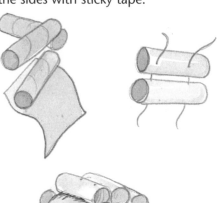

Ragdoll wig: cut a strip of sticky tape about 10" (25cm) long - enough to stretch from forehead to nape of neck. Attach lengths of thick wool all along it, so that the tape is completely hidden. You can plait the wool if it's long enough, or else cut it into uneven lengths to make a shaggy wig. It will need to be held in place with a hairgrip.

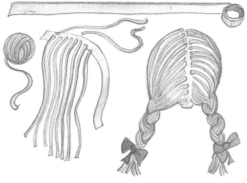

Paper curls: strips of paper curled round a pencil, or curling ribbon (the type used for gift wrap) make a very flamboyant wig. Use them instead of wool attached to the brim of your hat, or attach them thickly to a paper skullcap pinned to the hair.

JEWELLERY

If you and your children enjoy making props and accessories for costumes, then jewellery gives you the opportunity to have some real fun. Standard equipment can include cardboard, all-purpose glue, string, coloured foils and cellophanes (sweet wrappers, for instance), colourful magazine pages, drinking straws, gold and silver paint. Anything, really, which can be cut up, rolled, scrunched and painted to be transformed into priceless gems!

Brooches and buckles: cut a base design out of firm card. Spread a layer of glue, then make a design over it with loops of string, crumpled knobs of paper and drinking-straw edges. Allow to dry in place with a weight on top. Paint the brooch liberally with silver paint (spray might be easiest, though more expensive) and allow to dry.

Bead necklaces: you can make your own beads from tightly-rolled and glued magazine pages, chopped into $^3/_4$ inch (2cm) lengths; alternatively, cut the pages into long, thin triangles and roll up individually over a knitting pin, starting at the widest edge. Secure with a spot of glue. Or use macaroni. Or look for plastic beads on sale cheaply at your local market or charity shop. Make several strands to wear together - separately or twisted. Buttons can also make a good substitute for beads, especially those with one or two holes (rather than a shank). Thread the string through two holes and the buttons will lie flat, side by side.

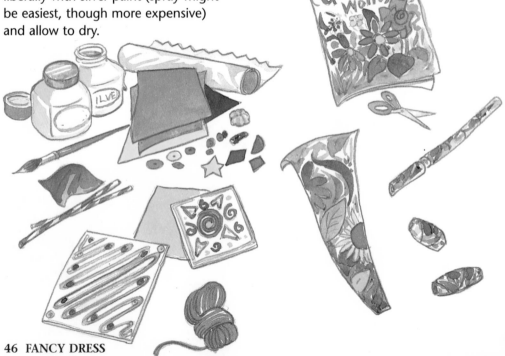

KNIVES AND SWORDS

Ideally use toy versions to go with your costumes: on no account use real ones, however sensible you consider your child. If necessary, make your own from card, covered with foil or silver paint.

Young children can make do with a straightforward, flat sword shape with a blunt point. Older ones (and the Dragon Slayer) might need something a little more sophisticated. Wind string tightly round the hilt to give it more substance.

You can make a more realistic hilt with three ping-pong balls and cardboard tubing (see diagram).

Paint silver and add foil 'jewels' at the centre to disguise the join of the two tubes. To make the blade a little fancier, apply a pattern of string (like the brooches described earlier) to the top part of it, sprayed silver.

A knife wound: make a cardboard knife but with the blade foreshortened at a slight angle, as shown. Make a slit in the centre of the bottom edge and fold back tabs in different directions. Push the knife through a suitable slit in your shirt and tape the tabs securely against the back of the shirt. Paint a liberal amount of fake blood round the wound. Writhe convincingly.

FACE PAINTING

Face painting has quite a magical ability to draw children out of themselves and into the character they have become. It's not surprising that the technique has been in use for thousands of years! There are a number of excellent books available on the subject to give you ideas and designs to follow, and you might find it worthwhile to invest in some basic equipment, like soft sponges and a range of paintbrushes, to help you achieve better results.

Here are suggested designs for some of the characters in this collection, to give you inspiration.

Safety note

Always use water-based face paints. Test them first by applying a small patch on the inside of your model's wrist. If there is no allergic reaction after a couple of hours, then they should be safe to use.